Say It In Crucian!

A complete guide to today's Crucian for speakers of Standard English

Me vex!

I tellin yo!

By Robin Sterns

Antilles Press
4093 Diamond Ruby #127
Christiansted, U.S. Virgin Islands 00820

ISBN: 978-0-916611-06-4

Graphic design by Robin Sterns, Intelligent Design.
Typeset in Tequila, Giddyup, Schnitzle, Damaged Guts and Century Schoolbook.
Images © Fotolia and istockphoto.

Printed by Alexander's, Linden, Utah.

See companion website:
www.cruciandictionary.com

Contact us:
cruciandictionary@gmail.com

ANTILLES PRESS

✳ Table of Contents

About this Book ✳

This book began as a nefarious plot, a typical English teacher ploy to get her terminally bored students to focus on the grammar and structure—and ultimately, the beauty—of their native language.

I've been engaged in some version of this plot at various universities for nearly 30 years, and it became much more interesting when I returned in 2005 to the University of the Virgin Islands St. Croix campus, where most of my students could "code-switch" effortlessly between Crucian and Standard English. Many also speak several other languages and creoles. I decided to alter my research-writing course so students could research and write about their language uses (while I was secretly honing their Standard English).

Eventually I realized I was learning at least as much as they were. Crucian is not simply "broken English," as some of my students call it. It is a rich language full of wit and irony and wise expressions. I was surprised to learn that there are things you simply cannot express as well in any other language.

Many linguists see Virgin Islands Creole as a dying language, one that has been infected by words and expressions from the Americans and natives of other Caribbean islands who have moved here, the push toward Standard English as the language of education and financial success, the influences of cable TV, movies and the Internet.

But Crucian dialect, or "raw Crucian" or even "Cruzonics" as my students refer to it, is still a very popular means of communication. Tune in to Isle 95 and you'll hear deejays and callers speaking a mash-up of Crucian, stateside urban slang, Spanish and Spanglish, with a sprinkling of patois tossed in the kallaloo. Young people text Crucian; they've made groups devoted to it on Facebook.

Eventually I realized I could expand the classroom assignments into research in intercultural communication, and one result is this book, which offers a window into this culture and these people for those who aren't familiar with it, through the words and ideas of St. Croix's young people.

Another is the companion website, cruciandictionary.com, which allows people everywhere to learn about today's Crucian and add words and phrases as they become current.

This book is not intended as a definitive linguistics or dictionary. It is a snapshot of St. Croix and its youth at this moment in time from the point of view of someone from somewhere else who loves living here, and who sees the connection to everything that language is.

Most people who live here speak Crucian effortlessly, but it can be difficult for visitors or new residents to understand and take a long time to acquire. This book is for you, to help you develop the ear for this language, so that hopefully very soon when you are standing in the interminable line at the Kingshill Post Office and someone cracks a joke that makes the whole place fall out, you'll be laughing too.

Robin Sterns

St. Croix - November 2008

*what are they saying?
use the dictionary starting on p. 70
to look up crucian words and phrases
or see complete standard English
translations, p. 64!

Note on Spellings

Since Crucian is a largely oral rather than written language, there is no standard spelling (people don't even agree on how to spell "Crucian"). For a single expression (take "Me ain know," Crucian for "I don't know"), one native speaker might separate the words into Standard English-like equivalents in written form ("Me ain't know"), while another might write "meaino" or "meeno," which is much more like it is pronounced.

This guide is designed to make it as easy as possible for the non-native speaker to communicate in Crucian, but be aware that if you point to a question or phrase in this book, the native speaker may be just as confused as you are.

Note on Usage

Crucian is not the language of education or commerce; it's the language of gossip and storytelling and everyday conversation. The Crucian in this book is used by young people: older Crucians might not use or understand some of these expressions. Some of the expressions in this book might be perceived as—or ARE—inappropriate, rude or even offensive in some contexts, so use your judgment.

Pronunciation

Compared to Standard English (SE), here are some Crucian (C) pronunciation differences:

"th" sound = "d" or "t"
    (SE) three = (C) tree   think = tink
    that = dat   they = dey
    mouth = mout

The suffix "er" = "a" or "ah"
    later = latah   sister - sistah, sista
    after = afta   water - watah

The suffix "ther" = "duh" or "dah"
    other = udduh   father = faddah
    mother = muddah corner = cornah

Words ending in consonant sounds, like "t" or "ve" - the final consonant sound is often dropped and the word runs into the next one.
    give her - gishe
    let's go - leh we go
    Get away from here - Geh from ya.
    turn left - Tuun lef
    west - wes ("She live in Wes" = "She lives in the West/
        Frederiksted side of the island")

could - co, cou
care - in Crucian, rhymes with "ear" ("Me ain care")

Some words have a "y" sound added:
car - cyar
girl - gyul, gyal
boy - bwai, bwoy
carry - cyarry
cat - cyat

Crass or rude words may have a letter or two added or changed, seemingly to soften the negative effect:
ass = rass
stupid = strupid, shupid, chupid

Everyday Phrases

Greetings

Babylon?? What's that mean?!? check the dictionary starting on p. 70 to find out!

On St. Croix, you never just jump in and ask for something you want in a store or other business setting the way you would back in Babylon. This is considered incredibly rude and may result in less than satisfactory results. You might not get any response at all, or you may be cut off with the appropriate greeting, delivered in a tone of admonishment. You might even hear, "What, I woke up with you this morning???", suggesting tartly that only THAT would justify your lack of greeting.

So, in all situations, begin with a greeting, generally related to the time of day. If it's anywhere near a holiday, express appropriate holiday wishes as well. Plan on a couple of greetings before getting around to the point of your conversation.

In social settings, say, in arriving at your favorite beach bar for a sunset cocktail, plan on greeting everyone in sight, even people you don't know. Dat gon separate yoh from deh touriss-dem, who can be rude-rude!

Good morning = "Good mahnin"

"Good afternoon" - (used starting at the stroke of noon—
    people sometimes check their watch or a clock to see if

the greeting has officially moved from "good morning" to "good afternoon.")

"Good evening" - (from around dusk, 5 p.m.ish, to full dark)

"Good night" - (On St. Croix, this is a greeting, not an end to the conversation, used after dark)

"Alright" or "Alright, alright" - (an informal greeting, appropriate anytime)

"Irie" (eye-REE) - from Rastafarian, meaning everything is fine, a good vibe

(SE) How are you?
(C) "Ya safe?"   "You safe o what?"
"How you DOin?"   "Wha ya sayin?"
"Wha goin on?" (run together, like "whaGOinon," not
necessarily asked with an inflection at the end)
"Hail up."

I'm fine.
"I safe, dehman.   "I bin fine."
"I'm fine, an yoh?" (and you?)
"Yes I." (To mean "safe," "cool," I'll see you.")

Expressing surprise/disbelief:
"Whaa?"
"How you mean?" = "I beg to differ." Said in a
challenging tone: ("HOW you mean!")
"Eh-eh" = akin to American "Uh-oh."
"Cheese and bread!"
"Well, my peace!"

Crucian
Cinderella
by Miguelina Valdes

With convenient Standard English translation

Expressing agreement:
    "meSON?"   "Ooh lawd!"
    "I tellin yoh!"   "Thank you!"

Expressing disagreement:
    "Neva dat."   "Nah dat deh."
    "Me ain tink so."   "T'all" (not at all)

Social Conversations

(SE) Where are you?
(C) "Wha pah you deh?"

Where is he/she?
"Wha pah he/she deh?"

Where are you going?
"Pah you goin?"

Is he going to meet you there?
"He gon meet you dere?"

Where was that?
"Weh dat deh bin?"

Have you eaten?
"You done eat?"

Well, once upon a time, right? day had a lil gyal by deh name of Cinderella. She wa living alright wit her fada.

Once upon a time, there was a young girl named Cinderella who happily lived with her widowed father.

→

Do you understand?
"You check?"

Do you speak American English?
"You duh speak Yankee?"

Do you speak Crucian?
"You duh talk Crucian?"

I can't speak Crucian.
"I duh speak Yankee alone."

Eh geh a jam in wes, ya goin?

Wha pah in wes?

In Whim. Tings gon get wild.

Alright, chek you latah!

Her fada wa lonely so he geh married to dis big hefa, who come wit her two datas who tink day bin hot!

Her father was lonely, so he married a beautiful but cruel woman, who brought into the household her two daughters, also beautiful but evil-hearted and conceited.

I don't understand a word you're saying.
"Me ain unnastan a ting yoh saying mehson."

What's up? What's going on?
"Wha you sayin?"
"Wha you dealin with?"

Let's go.
"Leh we go nuh."

What day is it?
"Wah today be?"

I'll be back later.
"I gone to come back."

I'm leaving.
"I gan from yah."

Come here.
"Come ya."
"Chek ya."

Q: Do you mean it?
"Fah true?"

See you later!
"Check yah latah!"
"We'll link up you latah."

A: I'm serious! (I do mean it)
"Seerias!"

Dem deh taght dat day run tings in deh house, so shrupid Cinderella become a slave.

The cruel stepmother and her daughters took over the household, treating poor, unassertive Cinderella like a lowly servant.

Family Relationships

Family relationships are of great interest to Crucians, and central to getting things done expeditiously on St. Croix.

"Who he be to you?"
(What is the family relationship? How is he related?)

Flirting

Flirting is a serious test of linguistic dexterity in the Caribbean. On St. Croix, flirtatious remarks ("lyrics") are designed as much to highlight the verbal wit of the flirter as compliment the flirtee. A proper positive response is to subtly acknowledge the wit, perhaps with a small smile, and move on. To discourage the flirter, chupse (see page 21) and move on. When you're really brave, you can throw a retort back and see what happens next.

I tink she foget dat Queen Mary buun down bush, houses, and everyting she find in her way to help we geh free from slavery.

Cinderella must have forgotten that Queen Mary led the 1878 Fireburn on St. Croix to put an end to unfair labor practices and guarantee real freedom for former slaves.

Flirter

"Miss, yoh gah a license for dat wais?" (a license for that waist, meaning 'can the way you move possibly be legal?')

"You sharp, yah." = "You look really good."

Retort

"I bin hearin the music but I ain dance yet!" (meaning 'talk is cheap - where's the action?')

In dat village it had a sexy ting who wa single and he wa lookin fo a woman, ya check?

In the community lived a handsome young man who was interested in romancing a young woman.

dealin = unofficially dating
deh togeda = "they're together," officially dating
coop, coopin = to "check out," look at someone closely
pop style, poppin' style = he or she is looking good
cuttin' style = acting snobbish, refusing to flirt back

Whe ayo waan go? Leh we go azick tonight!

Leh we go Moonraker.

No man, ova deh does get too much fight. Leh we go coop dem lock-up dudes by Club Passion.

So he tell everybody come ova to his house fo dis jam to find deh perfect woman, not the perfect gold digga.

He invited everyone to a swinging party at his residence in hopes of locating a suitable love interest.

Disagreements

"Meh vex" = "I'm upset."

"He dah buun me." = "He burns me up/ticks me off."

"Bax dung he rass."

"Cuff he upside he head."

"You sick de man?" = "Are you crazy?"

"Ah cyan stan yorass" = "I don't like you."

"Me ain tekin dat" = "I'm going to hit you back."

"Move from ya" = "Get away from here."

"Ah good!" = "Serves you right!"

"You doan done." = "You just won't quit."

Siddong before I drive yoh rass some hard slap!

Scatta yo baxide! You doan done.

Well, Cinderella sista dem went playin briss and leave shupid Cinderella behind mopping up deh floor dem.

Cinderella's evil stepsisters decided to attend the party and leave poor Cinderella behind to clean up after them.

Humor

Crucians have a great sense of humor, witty and dry. It often pokes fun at people's foibles, and Crucians love to make plays on words. Watch it, though. When an outsider is around, the Crucian can get pretty thick, and the joke may be on you!

Here's a true story that illustrates Crucian humor. I had just finished taking the written drivers' test at Public Safety and got in line to pay the cashier. I could tell right away, though, there was some kind of problem:

Man #1: "I tink I make she mad. Or maybe twas you."
    [pointing to another man in line]
Man #2: [shrugs]
Me: "What's going on?"
Man #1: "She decide she ain wukkin no more."
Man #2: "Miss! Miss!" [calling through the hole in the cashier's plexiglass]. "Miss, please take my money so I can go home!"
Cashier: [appearing at the window] "I done for deh day. I got a meeting tree o'clock an I cyan do no more work."
    [She shuts the window. It's 2:20]
Man #1: "Chuupse. She meeting mus be on St. Thomas."
Man #2: "She probly gettin Ployee uh de Month."

I wa in shock when I hear dat Cinderella had stitch up she dress to go, but dem damn gyal bruk it up so she don go nowhere.

Cinderella sewed a dress to wear to the party, but her evil step-sisters ripped it to shreds so she would not be able to attend.

 Nonverbal Communication

Chupsing/sucking teeth

The single most important nonverbal expression on St. Croix is "chupsing," sucking teeth to indicate disapproval or disagreement. Want to hear it? Just get yourself into a slow-moving line at K-Mart or Cost-U-Less. But don't "chupse" at an older person: that's RUDE.

A great definition:

"The sound made by pouting and sucking one's teeth in a manner probably African in origin but which, among West Indians, has been elevated to a minor art form. It is used by both sexes of all ages from puberty onwards, and knows no social, class or colour barriers. It provides a distinctive, wordless and highly expressive way of indicating anything from extreme annoyance, through incredulous disbelief, disgust and indignation, to amused tolerance and self-reproach."

Source: Dyde, Brian. Caribbean Companion: The A to Z Reference. London: MacMillan Press, 1993.

Cinderella start to cry an cry, until some jumbie come up outta de ceiling. Dis one bin a nice jumbie.

Cinderella cried unconsolably until a kind spirit materialized, right before her very eyes.

21

Finger pop
Making a popping sound by flicking one's thumb against one's middle finger, usually a grand gesture, to express agreement or punctuate a statement. It's sort of like snapping your fingers (the gesture used by statesiders to acknowledge the beat in music, for example), but more expressive.

Head nod
Making eye contact with another person (or the driver of another vehicle) and nodding your head up slightly, leading with the chin, says, "I acknowledge your presence. Hello!"

Cut-eye: a mean or disdainful look
Response to cut-eye:
"Wha I do you?" = "What did I do to you?"
"Wha happen to me now?" = "What did I do to make you mad?"

Sweet-eye: A flirtatious look
"Dah boy flashin sweet-eye at me!" = "That boy is winking at me."

Long-eye: A greedy look
"Your eye long, dehman."

Dat jumbie hook up de gyal from head to toe, he do some spell deh and she had a prettier dress dan deh one she had before!

The spirit cast a spell and she was instantly dressed from head to toe, including a frock even more stunning than the one the stepsisters had destroyed.

Gurl, u won believe wah I bout 2 tell u. I was at school waitin 4 my muddah an she wah tekin long, I wah so vex ain even funny. And then she roll up drivin a new bile, I was like, 'wow whah pah u deh car from,' an she ask me if I like it? I wah like 'of course I like it.' She goin tell me 'well this your new bile,' I was 'stop lie,' and she was 'it's yours.' Gyurl, I scream down tha place like I was a mad woman!

Gyal even geh her rims-up carriage, wit her brand new off-deh-market Gucci glass slipas.

The spirit even gave her a spectacular carriage to travel to the party in and a beautiful pair of glass slippers.

Being Polite ✳

Native and transplanted Crucians alike have extremely high standards for politeness. It's easy to appear rude even when you are behaving in a way that would be polite enough at home. Make eye contact, acknowledge the presence of others, and watch what's going on around you. Is your dinner taking forever to arrive? Well, so is everyone else's! So cool out mehson.

Being Polite in Your Car

Listen to other drivers as they tap their horns. A subtle beep! beep! is how we indicate any number of things, from "Thanks for letting me in traffic" to "I know you!" to "I'd like to get to know you." The only people who lay on the horn are drivers of large, heavily-loaded trucks, the message being, "Don't even THINK of pulling out in front of me." This is advice best heeded.

Stopping to Chat

In town, and even on roads outside of town, it is not at

Our famous Diamond Gyal helpas do up her head, cause gyal head had nappy!

Skilled attendants from St. Croix's famous Diamond Girl Beauty Supply appeared to style her hair.

all unusual for someone in front of you to stop smack in the middle of the road for a little conversation, to admire a particularly nice tuna hanging from a tree, or because we got a cell phone call and don't want to be out of

Gyurlfren if u had see dem man in dem tights at deh track meet. Good God almighty! U woulda bin drooling jus like how I did. And u could done see who got to who's not, dem dey wi dey Speedo suits. And dey had some foine brothas too. U shoulda see dem sexy Puerto Rican papis. I wish you was de wi me.

She ain had no damn rats as her horses dem, she had our locally owned horses from deh race track.

Unlike the Cinderella in the old-fashioned failytale, who had to settle for rats to pull her carriage, Crucian Cinderella had beautiful thoroughbreds from the Randall 'Doc' James Racetrack.

compliance with the law. This can be a bit disconcerting to the person right behind them when it happens. Look for the driver's left arm and hand to make a repeated "down, down" motion to indicate anything from "I'm stopping" to "I'm turning up ahead" to "Slow down: there's a herd of goats in the road."

Deh po-po stop me and say 'Is eida yo tek off deh tint dem, or tek a ticket.'

Dat police from dung de road, he punky muddaskunt come with he gun and going tell me my tint too dark and I need tek it off.

Yoh ain hear she had to be home by twelve, so she had to reach deh quick to geh it goin on.

Unfortunately, Cinderella had to be home by midnight, so she arrived at the party as soon as she could.

Right of Way

This is the most difficult concept for newcomers to understand, and at the same time the most indicative of the generous spirit of Crucian culture. Many people think of right of way as meaning the driver with it gets to go. It's the opposite here. Here, the driver with right of way looks for opportunities to yield it. So, for example, it's common for through traffic on Centerline Road to come to a halt while folks on a side road (who would otherwise be sitting there all day) get a chance to join the throng.

People turning off main roads often stop to let out side-road traffic before making their turn. They indicate yielding by waggling their fingers in a "come, come" gesture or by flashing their headlights.

The ultimate in yielding right of way is when drivers on both sides of a main road plan to make turns after letting out the side-road traffic. When this complicated maneuver works properly, it is a delicate ballet of yielding in turn (drivers on the side road go first, then the driver who must cross a lane of traffic to turn, and finally the person who could have simply turned onto the side road in the first place).

Well, when gyal reach, all dem hatas eyes bin on she!

When she made her entrance, jealous people, including the evil stepsisters, couldn't take their eyes off of her!

Food ✳

Once I was in a line at the Frederiksted Kentucky Fried Chicken (we call it "Kentucky" here), at high noon, when they ran out of chicken. We were informed of this by a young lady who came out to address the line, announcing, arms akimbo, "Chicken finish." "Finish," by the way, is pronounced with the emphasis on the end of the word, "Chicken finISHHH." Could anything express finality more clearly than that? Mean tink so.

Helpful restaurant expressions

(SE) A table for two, please?
(C) "We cou siddong?"

Can I have some of that?
"I co geh some of dat?"

Could I have some water?
"I co geh some watah?"

Are you thirsty?/I'm thirsty.
"You tusty?/I tusty."

Do you accept credit cards?
"Yoh tek credit cahd, yah?"
"Yoh ain take credit cards?"

How much does that cost?
"How much dat deh be?"

Gyal cack up she bana and swing it from lef to right. Boy, dem hatas was vex!

She started dancing very fetchingly, much to the dismay of those who were jealous of her.

I am not eating anything.
"Me ain eating nutting."

I would like a Heineken, please.
"Green beer now man!"

I do not have any.
"I ain geh none."

What do I owe you?
"How much I have for you?"

The sun does be blazin hot so I tink I waan tek a dip in de watah.

Wheh deh sunscreen be? Sun hot-hot an me ain self waan geh buun!

Deh sexy ting look at she and had done what she want from deh beginning, well you know women does play hahd to geh.

The handsome young host observed her performance and was mesmerized, which is what she had desired all along, even if she initally had feigned disinterest.

✳ Advanced Crucian: A Basic Linguistics

Okay, so you've been on island long enough that you're starting to understand Crucians when they're talking among themselves. Maybe you're even developing an understanding of Crucian wit. Maybe you've mastered a few simple expressions yourself (you'd be surprised how much mileage you can get from just a couple of them. My personal favorites are "me ain know," delivered with a shrug, guaranteed to bring a meeting-roomful of high-flown academics to a standstill, and the challenge "How you mean?!?," an expression singularly brilliant for its clarity and seemingly utter ungrammaticality wrapped up in one little three-word package).

Now it's time to work on really speaking the language.

What follows is no definitive guide: for one thing, this is an oral language, with no set spellings and looser sentence structure options than a formal language like, say, French. For another, my sources are college students, so what you see here is peppered with slang and topics of interest to young people. Some of it is deliciously crass.

He start up wit his lyrics dem, and she fall fo dem.

He flirted with her shamelessly, and she succumbed to his charm.

It may be impossible for you to pass yourself off as a native speaker, but use the following to help develop your ear and your facility with this wonderful means of communication.

Forming Declarative Sentences

In Standard English, simple declarative sentences follow the pattern S + V + O, subject first, then verb, then object: "He threw the ball." = He (S) threw (V) the ball (O).
"I go to school."
"I see her."

The same is true in Crucian, although articles (like "the" or "a") may be altered or missing and objects don't necessarily take the same forms as they do in Standard English (See "Subjective and Objective Pronouns," p. 41).
"He had trow deh ball."
"I goh school."
"I see she."

Tis wa midnight and Apostle bin playin "Day Cyan Hold I Down" and ya damn right ain nobody coulda hold down Cinderella.

At the stroke of midnight, the famous Crucian Reggae musician De Apostle was singing his hit song, "They Can't Hold Me Down," and it was as if the song had been written just for Cinderella.

✳ "There is" Constructions

In Standard English, we use "there is/are" constructions often in declarative sentences.
"There are four girls in the class."
"There is a large tree at the corner."
"There was a long wait for tickets."

Crucians tend to substitute "it have/had" or "eh geh":
"Back in dem days, it had dis gyul name Cinderella."
"Eh geh a jam in Wes."

One time I asked a group of students if they thought Othello, Shakespeare's tragic hero who killed his true love in a jealous rage, could exist today on St. Croix. "It have Othello like peas!", one student asserted. "There are Othellos everywhere you look," she was saying.

Forming Questions ✳

In Standard English, there are several ways to form

Gyal run, and leave her Gucci slippa behin.

She exited the party so swiftly that she failed to retrieve her glass slippers.

questions. One is to reverse the order of the subject and verb:

Declarative sentence: "I am late."

Question: "Am I late?"

Thank goodness she reach home, buh gyal ain gon foget dat kiss and dat night.

She made it home safely, and it was a night - and a kiss - she would never forget.

The same form can be found in Crucian:
"Who da be?" - "Who is that?"

A second option in both Standard English and Crucian
– although much more common in Crucian – is to leave the
sentence in its declarative form but add a question mark
and rising inflection in the voice:
Declarative: "I'm late."
Question: "I'm late?"

In Standard English this form often indicates surprise
("How can I be late?") or irony ("You think I'M late
- what about YOU?").

In Crucian, adding the question mark and inflection is a
very common way to form questions:
"He fraid?" = "Is he afraid?"
"I cou get some watah?"

Another common way to form questions in Crucian is in
the negative. The sentence is framed negatively, but the
intention is positive.

Bruddaman bin hook on dis gyal and
went around whole town lookin fo
Cinderella.

The handsome young man was utterly smitten and searched
the entire community for Cinderella.

"You ain fraid ah he?" = "Are you afraid of him?"

"You ain waan go deh?"= "Do you want to go there?"

"You ain going to deh movies wih me tonight?"

"You ain hungry?" - you answer "yes" if you are, "no" if you aren't.

Forming Negatives

In Standard English, we look for words like "not" and "no" to indicate negativity.

"I am not a singer."

"He's no singer."

"He isn't [is not] here."

Negative sentences in Crucian usually employ "ain't" and/or "no."

"Why you no buy dem?" = "Why didn't you buy/aren't you buying them?"

"Me ain know you does wuk deh." = "I didn't know you work there."

Finally, he reach to Cinderella house and dem ugly sistas a Cinderella try on deh slippa.

At last he came to Cinderella's house, where the hateful stepsisters insisted on trying on the glass slipper.

Sometimes, Crucian employs double negatives, which are frowned upon in Standard English:

"I ain no singer" = "I am not a singer."

"Nuh weain see nutting like dat deh." = "No, we didn't see anything like that."

"Me aint want no ticket." = "I didn't want to get a ticket."

Forming Plurals

In Standard English, we generally add "s" or "es" to form plurals. So "boy" becomes "boys," while "box" becomes "boxes." There are exceptions, such as "child" becoming "children" and "man" becoming "men."

Crucians generally use the word "dem" ("them") to indicate plurals. So "books" is "book dem." As Crucians are more and more impacted by Standard English, the forms can be combined ("books dem").

Crucian has exceptions too. Sometimes "dem" is used before the noun ("Look ah dem chair"). "All" can indicate

One a dem foot bin too fat and deh oda one bin too long.

One stepsister's foot was too wide to squeeze into the shoe, and the other one's was too long.

Mehson you aint going to believe wa happened to me today. This trick come steppin to me with a bunch of attitude when I was at work. So I tried to simma down and listen to wa the gyual had to say until she refer to me as 'you people.' I felt like slapping the curls out of her head. I was so vex but I still kept my cool. You know I had to handle the situation on a professional level or else there would of been a kalaloo up in the place.

Bout time Cinderella come out and ask, "I cou try it on?" When she try it on dat, it wa her size!

Just then, Cinderella emerged from the shadows and asked, "Could I try it on?" It fit her perfectly!

plural sometimes ("Look ah all de mango fallin out de mango tree deh deh ah Ms. Mable yard"). Crucians use "people dem" and "children dem."

"De chilren dem goin to school afta de dun clean de room."

"All de people dem in de street betta to move before de geh knack dung." ("...before they get knocked down")

Forming Possessives

In Standard English, possession is shown by adding an apostrophe and "s" to the end of a noun or pronoun. So to say that a book belongs to Anna, we say it's "Anna's book." If something belongs to more than one person, we generally put the apostrophe after the "s" that is already there, as in "boys' books."

In Crucian, the apostrophe and "s" are generally left off. So to say that a comb belongs to Francesca; it's "Das Francesca comb."

If Lusito's car is parked outside, it's "Lusito car de park outside."

Gyal get married and she lived happy afta dat, although her fada had dead cause deh damn hefa ge he a heart attack.

Cinderella and the handsome young man married and lived happily ever after, although her father died as a result of the evil stepmother's cruel treatment of him.

"Das dey wagon."
"Bryan broda ride to Jackie house."
"Dis wuz my mudda dress."

We also use possessive pronouns in Standard English: "It is mine," "It is his," "It is theirs."

Possessive pronouns exist in Crucian too. A Crucian might say "De phone is hers" or "the food is ours." "We" might be substituted for "our": "Das we ting."
Q: "Is dis dem dey car?" = "Is this their car?"
A: "No, dis is we own." = "No, it's ours."
Q: "I tink dis yor shoe." A: "Nuh, das yours."
"The dahg ate he dinnah."
"Dat belahng to she." = "That belongs to her."

Crucians often substitute "mines" for "mine," as in "De book is mines."
"Da car paak ova dere is mines."
"The keys is mines." = "The keys are mine."

Rememba, he who laugh last laugh best!

The moral of the story is that goodness is rewarded and evil punished. Gyal buy she some hata blockkas dehman!

Your boy bin coolin with a book in his hand, lookin all studious and shit, when this foine looking redbone started rollin on me. She bin frontin like she couldn't solve some problem, buh all da while she bin watchin me out da corner of her eye. So you dun know I had to show her I was a P.I.M.P. Peep game: this is how cris I break it down to her. I start by gettin real close to her like if I was tryn to see the problem. Then I solve it for her and she was all ova me giving me hugs an suh. Finally, she gets up an started gettin ready to go to her nex class buh I saw dat she had a fatty. So I trow her a couple of lines and geh she hooked man. Naturally your boy got the digits and we goin OUT Saturday fo sho.

"Dat book is mines," but "Dat deh is my book."
The word "own" is often added at the end of the sentence, such as "Das his/hers own" and "Tis mines own."

In Crucian, the phrase "for you" is sometimes used where a Standard English speaker would use "my" or "your."
Q: "Did ayo see my brown leather shoes?"
A: "No de man, we ain see noting fo you." = "We don't see anything of yours."

✳ Subjective and Objective Pronouns

In Standard English, use of subjective and objective pronouns is pretty clear cut. "I" is subjective, meaning the form used for the subject of a sentence, the person doing the action, while "me" is objective, the object of the action. He-him, she-her, they-them, etc.

Not so in Crucian. Subjective forms are used almost exclusively.
"I buy it fo she." = "I buy/bought it for her."
"I had hear from she." = "I heard from her."
"Leh we gane." = "Let's [let us] go."
"Wha duh wrang wih he meson?" - "What's wrong with him?"
"When you leavin give she deh keys."

Negative constructions are an exception. In these cases, sometimes the objective form is used when Standard

English calls for the subjective form:
"Me ain know." = "I don't know."
"Me ain like he." = "I don't like him."

A native Crucian warns, however, that there's a delicate balance here: pepper your language with too much "me" where "I" is called for in Standard English and you risk sounding like you are from another part of the Caribbean.

Tenses

Standard English clearly delineates when action occurs through different tenses. In present tense, "I am here." In past tense, "I was here." In future tense, "I will be here." In conditional tense, "I would be here."

Crucian is much simpler, in that nearly everything is expressed in present tense. So "I see she" can mean "I saw her."

Crucians sometimes use "had" to indicate past tense.
"I had hear from she."
"I wuh lookin good, so I ain had care."

"Bin" (been) can indicate past tense: ("Dis one ya bin a nice gyul." - "This one here was a nice girl.")
"You ain bin in K-Maat yestaday?"
"Somebady bin stealin."

"It had" can substitute for "there was": "One day it had a lil gyul name Shaquanda da wuz loss in de rain foress."

"Gon" (think "going to") can indicate future tense: "I gon hear from she."

Crucians may use Standard English future tense when indicating conditional tense. So when expressing that they "would" like something, you'll often hear they "will" like it.

Sometimes the language of Crucian tenses seemingly defies logic. For example:
"Dey ain gon built dat house." = "They are not going to [future tense] built [past tense] that house."

Continuing Action ✳

To indicate continuing action as opposed to action occuring now or at a particular point in time (grammarians call this tense "perfect continuous"), in Standard English we ask "Do you speak Spanish?", to mean "Are you capable of speaking Spanish/have you learned this language?" as opposed to "Are you speaking Spanish?", to mean "Are you speaking it at this moment in time?"
"Do you eat sushi?"
"I can drive on the left."

In Crucian, "does" (perhaps spelled and pronounced "da"

or "duh") is used when forming declarative sentences and questions about continuing action:

"You does speak Spanish?"

"You does eat saltfish?"

"You da speak Yankee?" = "Do you speak [American-style] English?"

"The sun duh be blazing hot!"

# Emphasis

In Standard English, we sometimes add tags to confirm or emphasize what we are saying. For example, the affirmation "I can sing" is strengthened when "can't I?" is added after it.

In Crucian, tags include "mehson," which can be placed at the beginning or ending of a sentence or even used alone. Another is "boy," or "bwoy": "I could sing, bwoy!"

Some others:

"Meain havin none ah dat, ya check?"

"Wha hahppin, right? [story follows] = "What happened is that...."

You done wi dat ting o wha?

"He gone fishin, no?"

"I late de man."

Another way Crucians indicate emphasis is to repeat a word two or even three times:

"I co smell de weed strang strang." = "I could smell

44

marijuana smoke very strongly."
"She goin on bad-bad-bad." = "She was making a terrible fuss."

Crucians sometimes use "You dun know" where a Standard English speaker would say "you know" or "you can be sure" ("So you dun know I throw she a couple of lines and geh she hooked man.")

"yoh ain know" - used where in Standard English "You won't believe" or "you'll never guess" might be used ("You ain know wha happen to me da uda day?")

"yoh doh hear!" - used where a speaker of Standard English might say "you haven't heard?" (Yoh doh hear! Weenie mash up his ride sick-sick on de highway.")

Near and Far ✳

In Standard English, we use "here" and there" to indicate proximity: "I am here." "He was there."

In Crucian it's the same concept, using "ya" and "deh."
"I deh deh." = "I am/was there."
"I deh yah." = "I am/was here."
"I deh ya coolin, you?" = "I'm here relaxing, and you?"

This is one of the most obvious differences between Crucian and St. Thomian dialects. On St. Croix, "I deh ya." On St. Thomas, "I deh here" (pronounced HEH).

November ah last year ih had a big ting on the island mehson. Tempo bin ya fo deh big birthday bashment. Everybody bin talking bout wa deh gon wear and who deh gon go with and all kinda ting before Tempo even reach ya. Back den I was wuking Urban Threadz and I cuh tell you people bin spending da papa fo dis ting. My boss even mek me wuk ovatime and I ain even wanted to. I woulda like to mek da papa but guess wa I was going Tempo too. Mehson 8 o' clock cum and dis man ain close deh store so I was like, wa happen man tis time to go. Deh man tun round and tell me money is wa mek a business so he ain closing so I seh yea well you stay ya cuz I going bout my business. But right before I leave you dun know I buy a bad Baby Phat fit da ain even deh out in deh store yet cuz you know I ain having no twin up deh. I reach on deh road to ge up deh and I bin in traffic fo like two hours deh man so you dun know I knitting. Afta da I move a lil ting, den deh popo dem start driving round sehing ain geh no more parking so park pa u deh. Deh funny ting bout da is I bin all deh way...

Body Parts

In Standard English, we have a left foot, a right foot, ankles and calves. We have arms, elbows, wrists and shoulders.

In Crucian, it's not so simple or specific. "He bruk he foot" might mean he injured his foot, a knee, a shin bone. It's the same with arms. "She got spot on she han" might be referring to one of her hands, her forearm, her elbow, her wrist, and so on.

...by deh Yatch Club. I wa vex but I seh you know wa I spend my papa and buy a bad fit so I going and show dem wa I buy, you check? I walk all deh way to Cramer's Park looking sexy of course but my foot dem bin burning me mehson. I reach deh and tings dun bin popping off but I mek da long walk wurt it. I hook up with my girl dem and we had we a ball. The show bin bad an so too. Me and my girl dem wuk our back, jump up and so, wave our flag and represent deh real way fo deh VI. We stay fo deh whole show and end up leaving deh musi 7 o' clock in deh marning. Deh funny ting bout leaving is da I had to walk all deh way back to deh car but guess wa I was still looking de bomb so I ain ha care.

A Crucian Short Story

This story was written by Anika Johnson, a student in my 2007 fiction writing class, and now a secondary English teacher at the St. Croix Educational Complex. It's not just a story that makes me nearly kill self wid laugh every time I read it — it's a tremendous example of how young people on St. Croix use language.

Visitation
by Anika Johnson

Today is the day of my last formal observation, which means that everything has to be in tip-top shape for my advisor slash mentor slash university supervisor, Ms. Charlington, who is coming to evaluate my performance in the classroom.

I have prepared this great lesson I call "The Truth Behind Conflict" that the kids are gonna love. First I'm having them copy the notes off the chalkboard. I have kept the notes brief to avoid any complaints from the darlings about too much writing and also to gain more points on my observation form.

I've been avoiding, for quite some time now, *Competency 26: Teacher must write legibly in manuscript and cursive on the chalkboard.* If I get too lengthy, my sentences start to go down hill and the angels are quick to point that out.

I can imagine Ayana now, screaming from the back of the classroom, "Ms. Carter, wha happen to yoh words dem? Deh fallin down Blue Mountain man."

Of course all the other beauties will join in cackling like the jubilant group they are. And me like the idiot off to the side, trying to hide my embarrassment, saying, "Bear with me, guys. I'll get better by June."

After they copy the notes, I'll play the audio version of the short story and have them follow along in their workbooks.

Ms. Charlington will love this technique. She's always going on and on, talking in her dreadfully nasal neutralized accent, "It is important that you address the various intelligences of these students. Remember, we don't all learn the same way."

Well, here you go, Hexy. I've got the inter- and the intrapersonal, the logical mathematical, the visual. And bringing up the rear is my skit satisfying the bodily kinesthetic slash movement intelligence. Yeah, I've got this down. These saints in uniform won't know what hit them.

The bell rings and the students are trickling in.

"Good afternoon, guys, come in and have a seat anywhere." I say this because the desks are arranged in a semi-circle fashion to aid in the dynamics of my lesson. After all, according to the objectives on my neatly typed lesson plan, we are to *(1) examine conflict in a short story with 100% accuracy and (2) analyze motivation and reaction of literary characters from the reading with 90% accuracy.*

I turn to the chatterbox posse, Maya, Skye, and Nicki. Those three definitely cannot sit together; they talk too much.

"Maya, sit over here today," I say, pointing at the desk nearest to me.

Maya blurts out, "Not me, I aint sitting nex to dem sketty girl from east end."

"Excuse me, are you crazy?"

"Ms. Carter, you beta move me fram dem cause somebody about to get slap."

"Hello, Hello, Hello!" I yell. "Nobody is getting slapped in here today. Now, Maya, sit where I told you to and stop all this rudeness."

She reluctantly sways over to the desk and slams her books down before she glances at me and rolls her eyes.

I think to myself, "Now this little wench better keep quiet and not ruin this observation for me, else I'll slap her little ass myself."

I don't think there is a problem. Maya was addressing her comments to two girls at the other end of the classroom. This must be some type of misunderstanding, because those girls are the most well behaved and smartest students in this class. Nina tends to get a little distracted by Moreen, but both of them are still way ahead of the all the other students.

The rest of class comes in, and I am eager to get started. I keep a close watch on Maya.

"Okay, everyone, look at the board and take about five minutes copying these notes. When you're finished, we will go over them together."

I watch the clock. I am about 15 minutes into the lesson and she has not arrived yet. Did I mix up the dates? Maybe she is late. Don't tell me she plans to miss what might probably be the best lesson yet.

"Maya, you read the first term."

She straightens her back, looks at the chalkboard and begins to read confidently. "There are four stages of plot—exposition, rising action, climax, and falling action, also known as resolution. The falling action is me kicking Nina down the steps and Moreen running before she geh kick too."

Nina jumps out of her chair, shouting, "Well try it nuh!"

"Cum den, you tink I fraid you!"

"Hey! Hey! Hey!" I yell, as I rush between them with my hands up like a referee.

"I am feeling some tension in this classroom. Now, whatever happened outside, we need to leave it outside. Understood?" I say sternly, glaring into their conceited little eyes.

Of course nobody answers me and the girls just look at each other, fiercely determined to have one of those Dodge City showdowns.

Who do they think they are coming in here with attitudes? I take a deep breath and go on asking them questions, trying to build up class participation for when Ms. Charlington arrives.

This time around I am determined to get a score of five for superior in *Competency 9: Teacher encourages interpersonal communication using effective questioning techniques to promote critical thinking.*

Critical thinking, alright. I am in front of this chalkboard thinking critically about putting my foot up one of these girls' ass if either one of them ruins it for me.

"Ms. Carter, watch out!" And that's all I hear before a water bottle comes flying across the room and hits Nina in the face.

"Tek dat, trick," yells Nicki.

Then Moreen jumps up, yelling "Dats all you could do? Stay fram far and fling ting? Yoh coward now, but you aint coward when you deh in deh batroom with Romeo, eh."

Before I know it, the four girls are squabbling on the floor, viciously pulling hair, and tearing off each other's clothing.

"Stop it. Loose her. Please!" That's all I can say

while I am trying to pull Maya off of Moreen.

No amount of screaming on my part or the girls' stops this rumble. The other students are yelling, "Beat hah! Beat hah!" and the beads of sweat that formed on my forehead are now pouring down my face.

How could this happen? Please, Ms. Charlington, don't come. Please let me get home to find a message on my machine from you, saying you had an emergency and you could not make it.

Monitors finally come and they manage to break the girls apart and drag them outside.

Maya is yelling, "Aint done, yoh nuh! Wait, wait I gone geh you!"

I can't believe this. How ironic is it that my lesson today was based on conflict and the motivation behind a character's need to engage in it?

I look at the little devils, my eyebrows turned up, nose flaring open and lips tightly pressed. Some of them are sitting at their desks and others are fixing back the desks that were knocked over. Mark raises his hand and asks, "Ms. Carter, you okay?"

"No Mark, I am not. I was supposed to teach you about the two types of conflict and then you guys were supposed to act out a scene from the story showing conflict. Instead, you guys decided to create your own. Everyone take out a sheet of paper and answer this question: *What could the four characters have done to resolve the conflict? What was their motivation?"*

I hear footsteps at the door. I look up, and there is Ms. Charlington with her papers in one hand and bags in the other. Smiling, I say, "Oh, Ms. Charlington! You just missed our wonderful skit. The girls performed exceptionally well." 📖

You won't believe wah happen to we while walking to the bus shanty fo skool. Cuz we late, we decided to cut tru deh shawtcut in the bush. I had foget dah my fadda dankey bin in deh bush. Nex ting you know, we see deh stinking dankey eating grass right in deh way. So me an my brave self say, "Man, his stubborn self ain gon do we nuttin. Les hurry so we don miss deh bus." Buh guess wah, all of a sudden dankey just chawge afta we. We just stawt one screamin. I bin pullin Arianna cuh she jus freeze. Mehson, we run tru kasha tree, tan tan bush, and all kinda vines dah bin hangin from dah tambran tree. Den we see some half-dead ol man under deh same tree smoking he a piece a joint an had a Cruzan Rum in he han! We stawt one screamin again and jus end up runnin deh lang way to deh shanty. We ain miss deh bus, buh like you cou see, our sacks, shut and skyut full up a green stain and dry-up leaf! Dah dankey doh make me sick, yo hear?

Idioms and Proverbs ✳

Idioms

Idioms are commonly used expressions that cannot be understood from the literal, individual meanings of their elements. Standard English examples include "kicking the bucket" (meaning "to die") and "pounding the pavement" (meaning "searching for employment").

The following are some idioms in today's Crucian:

"All up in my sauce" - mind your own business ("Don get all up in my sauce!")

"Ayo ears long" - to be nosy or in other people's business.

Little Redz

A thrill-packed Crucian retelling of the classic fairytale

"broke like a dahg" - having no money at all ("I broke like a dahg, meson.")

"chicken head" - young women who are only interested in men for their money and nice cars ("I jus got a new whip and now all these chicken heads be sweating me.")

"Crucian time" - to be "on Crucian time" is to be late, often shockingly late, according to stateside standards. Certain events, such as the annual Crucian Christmas Festival parade, are famous for starting several hours late. As the saying goes, "On St. Croix, if you're half an hour late, you're 15 minutes early!"

"donkey years" - a very long time "(Meain see she in donkey years.")

Dey had dis gyal down the way dere and she was a ling hot gyal, buh one ting bout hah, she loved her old nene dearly. One day she was to carry a scale because her grandmodda needed deh herbs to heal a asthma. So Redz tell her nene she would check a partner to deal with dat vibez for hah. Her nene live way up yonder in the boondocks, past the rainforest in Frederiksted, so Redz had to use the back way through Grove to go to Mt. Pellier. On the way, in her bruk down put put 2-door Honda Civic, she stopped to the gas station to put gas. A rasta cum and start bupsing she for a ride in west and she say "hell "eat me out" - used to mean annoying or aggravating behavior (Boy, you does eat me out!")

"A face like a dropped pie" - very unattractive.

"Goat dress up as lamb" - a person putting on airs.

"Goat mout'" - Something someone says that comes true, usually something negative.

"Kill me dead" - expression to mean "knock me for a loop" or to be hilarious ("She does kill me dead!")

"Knock of the drum" - every party, every jam ("Look at she, she at every knock of the drum.")

no!" She had a suspicion the rasta was the drug lord name "Wolf" who everyone would talk about. Wolf wah peepin and skinning out just to see wah she had in the car because he had smell a scent of home-grown through the glass window. He ask her "Pah you goin?" She replied "By my nene cheap cuz she sick and geh asthma. I goin give she a remedy." So she hop in and went pah she business off to her nene house. At this, Wolf went with he fast ass and went through Frederiksted to beat her to her nene house. He wah just picturing on his way dere that big royal blunt he was cravin. When he reach to nene house he

"Like water (watah)"- (1) "to run your mouth like water" - talk too much, usually saying bad things about someone else ("Afta she had run her mouth like water I ask her if she was done."), (2) everywhere ("Babylon round de place like watah.")

"mash corn" - to set someone straight, put them down ("Ayo don wan to know whose corn I mash today!")

"off the chain" - from Stateside slang, used here to mean very cool, sexy ("That outfit is off the chain.")

"She too sharp for TV!" - when someone is too amazing or attractive for words.

knock and a screechin voice said, "Who is dah good-for-nuttin knocking on my door?" Wolf say "de man wid de remedy" so she fling open the door. At this time Redz came along in her put put and was like "Wah goin on ya! Wah de ras u doin by my nene house?" At this time, nene saw what Redz had bring she. She was so overwhelm she catch a asthma attack! Redz take out her tool and pump a shot in Wolf muddahscunt and he peel off down de road. She rush to her nene and use the bong as resuscitate de woman. When nene geh back on her feet she screamed to Redz, "Damn, dats some good shit!"

"Slow your roll" - have patience, calm down ("Yoh need to slow yoh roll meson!")

"pickin whelks" - Crucian equivalent for "high-water pants," wearing pants that are obviously too short.

"Throwing her words" - swearing.

"Wife" - sex ("I gon geh meh some wife.")

Proverbs

A proverb is a popular saying, usually metaphorical, that is thought to express a commonplace truth. A common Standard English example is "a stitch in time saves nine," meaning the sooner you tackle a problem, the easier it will be to fix.

Some common Crucian examples:

"Bragga was a good dahg, but Old Fast was better" - A person who brags a lot won't be as successful as someone who just gets the job done.

"bush ga ears" - "The bush has ears," be discreet.

"Belly full and bahna glad," "Belly full, bottom down" - a person who is full and satisfied after a meal.

"If yoh spit up in de air, e bound to fall back in yoh face"
= The wrong you do may come back to haunt you.

"Dag don need bone once" = If someone asks a favor of
you, you should do it because you might need one in the
future.

"Don give me a six for a nine" = don't do half the job, don't
cheat ("Wash my car good, don give me a six for a nine.")

"Goat head and sheep head noh one" = What seems quite
alike could be completely different.

"Hurry [or hungry] dag eat raw meat" = If you rush
something, you may end up spoiling the whole thing.

"If yoh noh hear lil bell, yoh bound foh hear big bell"
= One who does not listen will feel the consequences of
his/her actions.

"Knead the flour, now eat the bread" - equivalent to "You
made your bed, now lie in it."

"Monkey know wha tree to climb" = Every person knows
who to mess with.

"Nevah laugh when yoh bruddah geh wet" = Misfortune
has no favorites.

"Take yoh time, comb yoh hair" = wait, don't rush into something ("Chanelle, I see you watchin dem boys, but I beg you, take yoh time, comb yoh hair.")

"Time longer than twine" = Your bad deeds can catch up to you.

"What sweet in goat mouth sour in his behind!" - Goats will eat anything, including items they probably shouldn't, for which they may eventually suffer. Therefore, a person may appear to be enjoying himself only to pay for it later.

"When dag drink wattah, e tongue seh 'foh meh eh foh meh.'" = What is truly yours, no one can take away.

"What yoh buy, yoh wear" = Plant evil, reap evil.

"When yo dig yo hole, dig two" = Be careful what you plan for others so it doesn't come back to you.

"When yoh sorry foh magga hog, e tu'n 'round root yoh door" = Kindness does not necessarily bring kindness in return.

"When yoh yet yoh one, yoh hungry yoh one" = Give nothing, expect nothing.

"Who don't hear, does feel" = If you don't listen/pay attention, you'll suffer the consequences.

You ain know wha happen to me duh udda day? Well let me tell ya! I had just ge outa de business meetin when meh cousin Eric call meh up on meh cell phone tellin meh to com to dis bangin house paty. He wah tellin me how to find deh house when meh cell phone cut out, you know St. John ain neva geh no good signal, shitty Sprint company! Ah chupse meh teeth and I keep goin becas I taght I had enough of deh directions to fine deh house, buh I wrang and I ended up gein lost. Nex ting you know it start rainin and I sah these two white guys wakin up deh hill, so I stop an ask dem whe de goin. De tell me de goin to a house party, so I se ye it must be de same house party becase St. John aint gon have two house party in deh same night. So we gane, next thing you know de two idiot I pick up aint know whe de goin eida. So we like three jackass drivin up an down lookin fo a house we ain know whe pa e de. Mison! Da night we see pats ah St. John I neva taght existed. Afta about an howa we stop when one of the guys had a signal on his cell phone—mind you it was not a Sprint phone. So he call a fren that tell he whe de house be and guess what, it was right an tap ah deh hill we wah an, we all felt real schupit. My cousin Eric dun left, but I stay deh and let me tell you dem white people know how to paty mison!

Texting in Crucian

Today's young Crucians are no different from young people everywhere who have developed shortcuts for communicating via their cellphones, PDAs, on MySpace and Facebook.

Here are a couple of text conversations in Crucian. Much of what you see here is no different from texting elsewhere: "brb" for "be right back," "lol" for "laughing out loud" or "lmao" for "laughing my ass off." But there's a spice added to the mix when young people text message on St. Croix.

Conversation #1
Girl: wa go on?
Guy: I deh ya dread
Girl: right right dude I bored
Guy: Me too b...wa u want do?
Girl: meeno son I just have mi some kina fun...wanna go to isles?
Guy: no sa dread
Girl: You 4eva gone be a jackass
Guy: ah wa
Girl: yea b
Guy: no sa
Girl: lmao sick rass...well ttyl
Guy: lol aight...c ya

Conversation #2

Girl #1: hey girl, what up?

Girl #2: deh yah, chillin

Girl #1: wah goin on in Cruz?

Girl #2: same as always

Girl #1: so wah going on with the motherfucker [referring to Girl #2's boyfriend]?

Girl #2: he still trippin but you know how I does roll.

Girl #1: yea gyul, you is crazy

Girl #2: like fuck

Girl #1: lol

Girl #2: brb

Girl #1: yea

Girl #2: girl, I deh yah to work and I busy so halla at me latah

Girl #1: aight, we will talk laterz

Want to jump in? On Facebook, check out groups like:

I's a Crucian

I'd Rather be in St. Croix, USVI

I NEED MORE CRUZAN PEOPLE AT MY COLLEGE!!!!

You know u a Crucian when u are listenin 2 Isle95 on the internet..

You Know U From The Virgin Islands When U Speak This Language...

UVI Massive where you at!!!

I Like Chicken Leg and Johnny Cake!

Strictly Cruzan Rum

Area Code (3-4-0) MASSIVE!!!!

Translations

Here are Standard English translations for the Crucian conversations located throughout the book. Use the dictionary starting on page 70 to look up particular Crucian words and phrases.

Front Cover
"I understand there's a swinging party in Frederiksted."
"Let's attend it!"

Back Cover
"As I was clandestinely reading this book at work, I found myself laughing at my desk, resulting in my boss questioning my demeanor, but I paid no attention. This book is stupendous!"

p. 1
"I am annoyed!"
"I had noticed that."

p. 4
"Are you a Crucian?"
"Indeed, I was born here!"

p. 7
"I live in Frederiksted."
"Please don't attempt to fool me."

p. 9
"This new car is mine!"
"Wow, it looks great!"

p. 12
"There's going to be a party on the west end. Do you want to attend?"

"Where west?"

"In Whim. It should be a lot of fun."

"Alright, I'll see you later this evening!"

p. 15

"I suggest we find a quiet place to relax."

[sucks teeth] "I suggest you keep your distance!"

p. 16

"Let's go out tonight. Where do you want to go?"

"We could go to the Moonraker."

"That place can be a little wild. I'd prefer checking out the sweet-looking young guys with dreadlocks at Club Passion."

p. 17

"I suggest you back off before I am forced to engage you in physical violence."

"You should quit while you're ahead. You never give up."

p. 21

"You won't believe what I am about to tell you. I was waiting for my mother to pick me up from school. She was taking so long to arrive that I was getting upset. When she drove up, she was in a new car, and I asked her, 'Where is that new car from?' She asked me if I liked it, and I responded, 'Of course I do.' She then told me it was mine! I said, 'Don't tease me,' and she assured me the car really was for me. I responded with glee!"

p. 23

Girlfriend, if you had seen those male athletes in their tights at the track meet, you would have been as mesmerized as I was. You could even analyze the more personal elements of their physiques, because of their form-fitting outfits. In addition to their athletic prowess, some of the young men were very attractive as well, in particular a few of Puerto Rican descent. I wish you could have attended with me.

p. 24
"A policeman stopped me and said, "You either need to scrape the tint off of all of these windows or I will be forced to issue a ticket.""
"A policeman who lives in my neighborhood suggested that my tint was too dark and I need to take it off."
Note: On St. Croix we love our "tint," dark tinted windows that keep out annoying sunlight and prying eyes. In 2005, the V.I. Police outlawed tint darker than 35%. Many people failed the tint test and had to scrape dark tint off their windows. Resulting passions ran high.

p. 27
"The sun is so hot I think I'll go for a swim in the ocean."
"Do you know where the sunscreen is? I don't want to get a sunburn!"

p. 31
"Are you going to Wendy's later?"
"Unfortunately, I find myself with a severe cash-flow problem."

p. 35
"You won't believe what happened to me today. An unpleasant young woman approached me with a boisterous and negative attitude while I was at work today. I did my best to control my temper and listen to her problems, until she referred to me as "you people." This caused my blood to boil, but I was able to control my temper. Fortunately, I was

able to handle the situation like the consummate professional I am; otherwise, a physical altercation might have taken place."

p. 40
"There I was making a show of appearing studious with a book in my hand when an attractive light-skinned girl came by. She was pretending there was a math problem she couldn't solve, but she seemed to be flirting the whole time. Here's how I handled it: I began by increasing my proximity to her as if I needed to be close to see the problem. Then I solved it for her and received some grateful hugs in return. As she got up to go to her next class, I happened to observe her callipygous rear end, so I flirted with her a little more, ultimately reeling her in like a fine fish. I was able to obtain her phone number, and we have a date planned for Saturday."

pp. 44-45
"Last November there was a major party on island. Tempo [the TV channel] was here for their big birthday event. Everyone was talking about what they were going to wear and who they were going to attend it with, even before the representatives of Tempo arrived. At the time I was working at Urban Threadz, and I can tell you people were spending a lot of money for this party. We were so busy my boss made me work overtime, even though I didn't want to. I wanted to make the extra money, but nothing was going to make me miss that party. Before I knew it, it was 8 p.m. and my boss wasn't ready to close the store, so I reminded him it was time to leave. His response was that making money is what makes a business successful, and because he was making money he was not going to close the store. I responded that

his decision might apply to him but that I was on my way out the door. However, before leaving I bought a Baby Phat outfit that hadn't even been put out on display in the store yet, because I was not going to show up in the same clothes someone else at the party was wearing. I drove east toward the party, and I was in traffic for two hours so I was upset. Next, the police started telling us there wasn't any more parking near the party, so we should just pull over and park where we were. I was near the yacht club, which meant a long walk, so I was unhappy about it, but after I had spent all that money and bought such a fine outfit nothing was going to prevent me from showing it off. I walked all the way to Cramer's Park, looking sexy, even though my feet were killing me. When I reached the party it had already begun, and I made that long walk worth the effort. I found my girlfriends and we had a wonderful time. The show was great, and we danced and proudly waved our Virgin Islands flag. We stayed for the whole show and finally left at what must have been 7 a.m. Unfortunately I had to walk all the long way back to my car, but I was still looking fantastic, so it didn't bother me one bit."

p. 51
"You won't believe what happened to us while we were walking to the school bus stop. We were late, so we decided to talk a short-cut through the wilderness. I had forgotten that my father's donkey was back in there, and the next thing we knew, there was the donkey eating grass right in our way. I bravely said, 'He isn't going to do anything to us. Let's hurry so we don't miss the bus.' But all of a sudden the donkey came charging after us. We started screaming, and I had to pull Arianna along, because she was frozen in place. We ran

through acacia, leucaena and vines hanging from a tamarind tree. When we saw an old man under that tree smoking a marijuana cigarette and drinking from a bottle of Cruzan Rum, we started screaming again and ran all the way to the bus stop. We managed to make the bus, but as you might imagine, our socks, shirts and skirts were smeared with green stains and covered in dry leaves. That donkey makes me so mad."

p. 59
"Let me tell you what happened to me a few days ago. I had just finished a business meeting when my cousin Eric called my cell phone to tell me about a fun party. He was in the middle of telling me the directions to the house when my phone lost signal (the St. John area never has good signal for Sprint phones). I was under the impression that I understood where the house was well enough to find it so I kept going, but I was wrong and got lost. Next, it started raining, and I observed two Caucasian fellows walking up the hill. I stopped to ask where they were going, and when they said a party at a house in St. John I knew it had to be the same one. I offered them a ride, but it turned out they weren't clear on the directions either, so like three fools we drove around aimlessly for about an hour until one of them got signal on his cell phone—not Sprint, I'd like to point out—and a friend of his gave us directions. It turned out we were nearly there, which made us feel pretty stupid. It turned out that my cousin had left by the time I got there, but I stayed and partied with the Caucasian fellows, who turned out to be a lot of fun."

After page 59? You try translating! Use the dictionary starting on page 70 for help.

Dictionary of Today's Crucian

This dictionary contains Crucian words and phrases used by young people today, their definitions and pronunciations, Standard English equivalents and examples of usage as appropriate. Because there are no standard spellings in Crucian, be creative in your search: if a word starts with a "k" sound, check the c's as well as the k's. See also alternative spellings listed.

Is something wrong? Have words or phrases to add? Contact Crucian Dictionary at cruciandictionary@gmail.com and let us know.

A

abroad - used to describe anywhere that is not the U.S. Virgin Islands, including the U.S. mainland.

ah - "of" ("I geh two ah dem" = "I have two of them.")

aiight (awITE) - from urban slang, hipper way of saying "all right."

ain - literally, "ain't," used to indicate negatives like "am not," "are not," "is not," "do not," or does not" ("I ain do dat", "Me ain know", "Ayn my book.")
also: aiin, ayn, aint

allawe - "all of us" ("Leh allawe go.")
also: all a we, ahwe

anti-man, auntie-man - a gay person.

ariculcha - "agriculture," used to refer to the V.I. Dept. of Agriculture.

axe - pronunciation for "ask" ("I ain axin he dat.")
also: ax, aks

ayo - "all of you" ("Ayo wouldn't believe who harrassing me again.")
also: ayoh, ahyuh

azick - crazy, wild ("Leh we go azick tonight!")

B

"b" - from urban slang, reportedly a shortening of the word "brother," used to refer to a close friend.

babydaddy - from urban slang, the father of someone's baby (implies out of wedlock).

Babylon - from Rastafarian thought, in St. Croix used mainly to refer to America (often implying a strong but corrupt, immoral place), but also to anything that fits that definition, such as elements of local government or police. ("You betta be careful before Babylon roll up on you.")
also: Bab. See "The Bob."

bacchanal - to Standard English speakers, this is a wine-soaked party ancient Greeks and Romans used to have. To Crucians, this is a really great party in the present time.

back - refers to a man's back in relation to his sexual strength.
backhand - a slap

backside, baxide - "butt" or "ass" ("I gon kick he baxide.")

bahn - (pronounced BAHN) "born" ("I barn ya" = "I was born here.")
also: barn, ban yah

bal, ballin - (1) "to cry" ("He ballin now!", "She bawlin bout she purse missing"), (2) to flaunt money, to be noticably rich ("Since you ballin, buy me a car too.")
also: ball, bawl

"ballin up" - to roll marijuana into a loosely wrapped cigar.

"Bam!" - response to a stupid joke.
also: blam

bamboo - slang for penis.

bana - polite term for "rear end" ("She cack up she bana and swing it from lef to right" = "she danced", "If yoh don behave, I gon giyoh some good strap cross yoh baana.")
also: barna, bahna, baana

bangin - slang for exciting, wild, fun ("Ma cousin call meh up on meh cellphone tellin meh to come to dis bangin house pahty.")

bashment - party ("You ain gon deh big birthday bashment?")

bassidy, bossidy - not thinking straight/not acting logically, as a consequence of being in love or because it's raining heavily.

bachoom, batroom - pronunciation for "bathroom" ("One day in track I had to pee bad and I had planning to go and use my coach bachoom.")

bax - "box," hit. ("Bax dung he rass!")

bidness - slang for sex ("Afta dat we go her house and do our bidness.")

bile - short for "automobile" ("Then she roll up drivin a new bile, and I was like 'wow, wha pah you deh car from?'")

bin - literally "been," used for past tense "been" or "were" ("All dem hata's eyes bin on she.")

blak - "block," to ignore

blend - a separate leaf placed into a marijuana cigarette to bring a quicker high.

blinging - adaptation of Stateside slang for "flashy jewelry" ("She wah blingin like P. Diddy.")

Blue Mountain - At 1,100 feet in elevation, one of the tallest points on St. Croix.

blunt - marijuana cigarette ("He wah picturing that big royal blunt he was cravin.")

bong - a water pipe used in smoking marijuana

"boo-loo-loo" - refers to someone who is of large stature and seems to be clumsy ("This big boo-loo-loo man gone come and drap his nasty cigarette on my foot dem.")

bout - pronunciation for "about" ("Me ain know wha he takkin bout.")

"break it down" - to simplify for those unlikely to understand otherwise.

breed - pregnancy ("She leh he breed she" = "She let him get her pregnant.")

breed off - to impregnate someone/to action taken to become pregnant.

breeding - the state of being pregnant.

briss, brist - "nosey."

bruddah, bruddaman - brother, a man. also: broda, brodaman

bruk - break, broke.

bu, buh - pronunciation for "but" ("The foam party wa strupid, bu when we went over to Moonraker it was aiight.")

bupsing - asking, begging ("A rasta come and start bupsing she for a ride in west.")

bunnin, buunin - slang use of "burning," to mean smoking marijuana ("Ayo bunnin out ya?")

bush - wilderness (if there's such a thing on a small island), area of uncut brush ("We find dat we wah lost in de bush"), also used to indicate when a person or thing is missing ("He gone bush.")

bus, buss, "bust a lime" - relax, have fun ("Leh we go buss a lime.")

buss - bust, used to indicate taking action ("I buss he some kick," "He buss some dude a shot.")

"buss aff" - literally "bust off," to leave quickly ("We buss aff fo anywan had see" = "We hurried away before anyone saw.")
also: bus' off

"bussin it down" - breaking marijuana apart so it spreads around on the rolling paper better.

buun - (1) to be cheated, (2) smoke marijuana, or (3) be ticked off ("He da buun me!")

"buun tyas" - "burn tires," to make skid marks with the tires of a car.

bwai, bwoy - "boy."

C
cack - pronunciation for "cock" ("she cack up she bana" = "she cocked up her rear end.")

cah, cuh - pronunciation of "because" (I cyan go cah I sick bad, meson.")

cahn - literally "corn," used to refer to smoking marijuana.

carn - "cannot" or "can't" ("She carn drive.")

care (rhymes with "ear") - pronunciation for "care" ("Me ain care!")

chahcoal - pronunciation for "charcoal," can refer to a dark-skinned Black person.

check, chek - slang for "understand" ("ya check?") or "check out"/ listen to/experience ("Me gon check dis vibe", "Chek ya latah!")

"cheese and bread" - euphemism that substitutes for what might be a ruder expression of frustration ("Cyar registration line cyan done, meson. Cheese and bread!")

chi'ren, chilren - children.

chook - to poke or stab. also: jook

chupse - the act of pouting and sucking teeth simultaneously to express irritation or disagreement ("When my cellphone cut out ah chupse meh teeth and I keep goin.")
also: add as many u's as you like = chuuupse, chuups

"clear skin" - light-skinned Black person.

clung - "clown," used derisively ("Somebody tak to dis clung before he pickup some blows.")

cococs - a swelling on the head caused by a hit.

conny, cunny - rude slang for "vagina."

Cont'nental - Someone from the United States.

coolin - relaxing, doing just fine ("I jus deh ya coolin.")
also: koolin

coop, coup, coopin - staring at, observing closely, "checking out" ("He wuh coopin she.")

"crack head" - expression from Stateside urban slang to refer to a person who is addicted to crack cocaine.

crib - from urban slang, refers to one's domicile ("I jus came from the crib.")

cris - very nice, perfect, ideal ("Dat ride so new dah ting still lookin cris, de man"), can refer to a great sense of satisfaction ("After I see her I was feelin crist.")
also: kris, kriss, crist

Crucian - of St. Croix, U.S. Virgin Islands ("Crucian kallaloo") or a person born on the island. Some spell it "Cruzan"; others say "Cruzan refers to the rum, Crucian to the people." Sometimes pronounced more toward the "zh," as in "measure" or "azure"; sometimes more toward "sh," as in "sure." Never pronounced "z" as in "cruising."

crushing - to have a passing infatuation for ("I could tell she was crushing on me.")

crunk - from Stateside slang, a portmanteau word meaning crazy + drunk.

Cruz (CROOZ) - nickname for St. Croix, from "Santa Cruz" ("Yoh back in Cruz?")

Cruzonics - adapted from "Ebonics," Stateside term for African-American speech patterns. Used to refer to "youth Crucian."

cum - alternate spelling for "come."

current - used when Standard English speakers would say "electricity" ("WAPA cut de current.")

cyan, kyan - pronunciation of "cannot," "can't" ("She cyan reach in time," "I cyan stan deh gyul.")

"cyan done" - expression meaning endless supply or never ending ("At Carnival, deh food and libation cyan done.") also: can done

cyar - "car."

cyat - "cat."

D
"da bomb" - popular youth expression, borrowed from Stateside slang ("I wuh lookin da bomb, so I ain ha care.")

dah - "that."

dahtah - "daughter." also: data, datta

dag, dahg - pronunciation for "dog" ("De dahg took he bath.")

dain - "did not" or "didn't" ("We dain go.")

dankey - "donkey."

das, dass, dats - "that is/that's."

dat - "that."

dealin – when a couple is not yet officially dating, but are on their way to be ("Are you dealin wid he?")

de, de' - "the" ("See de tings dem right deh.")

dead - used to mean "die" and "died" ("Her fadda had dead.")

deh - "there/their" ("The girl deh unda deh tree", "It deh deh" = "It is there.")

deh man, dehman - used like "mehson" ("I late deh man" = "I'm late.")

dem - indicates plural. May come before the noun ("Look ah dem chair") or more often after ("He feed deh goat-dem", "de man dem ova dere.")

demde, dem deh - "they."

dem man - "those people."

"digits" - slang for "phone number" ("Naturally your boy got the digits an we goin out on Saturday fo sho.")

dingee - slow thinker.

doh - substitutes for "do" and "does" ("he doh talk Spanish?")

Dominicrucian - Crucian of Dominican Republic descent.

don - "do not" or "don't" ("I don sing.")

"donkey years" - a very long time ("He bin gone from ya donkey years.")

drap - pronunciation for "drop."

dread, dred - (1) can refer to a Rastafarian or someone who wears dreadlocks, (2) can be used as a slang form of emphasis at the end of a sentence ("I deh ya dread" = "I am here.")

dung - pronunciation for "down" ("We goin dung de road.")

dutty - "dirty."

E

eas - east, anything east of Sunny Isles ("He livin in Eas?")

eediot - pronunciation for "idiot," someone who continuously acts foolishly.

eida - (EEdah) "either."

enup - (enUP) pronunciation for "end up."

everyting - pronunciation for "everything."

F

faahm - (1) can be used to mean "woman," as in "femme" or (2) a general term like "thing" ("Before she know it, that fahm been 12 o'clock already", "We jus cruisin in dah park tryna tek pictures of Big Ben and dem fam.")
also: fam, faarm

faddah - "father."
also: fada

fatty - a big bahna (in a good way.)

fetch - "thing," used like "faarm" (Wha fetch I seein here?")

fit - slang for "outfit" ("You don know I buy a bad Baby Phat fit da ain even deh out in deh store yet" = "I bought a hot little outfit that wasn't even out on display yet in the store.")

flim - "film."

flit - "bug spray."

floupe - (pronounced FLOOP), a portmanteau word for "float" plus "troupe" that performs in the Crucian Christmas Festival parades.

flummoxing - "confusing" ("You flummoxing me?")

fo - pronunciation for "for," sometimes used when Standard English would call for "to" ("He gan fo cry all night" = "He cried all night.")
also: fa

"Fo wha?" - used to mean "Why do you ask?"

foget - "for getting" or "to get" ("She bin bout de age foget married.") also: fogeh

foine - slang for "fine," but pronounced with the "oi" of "voice."

foot - can mean "foot," but can refer to any part of the leg or the whole leg.

foolee - a complete idiot.

for - used where a Standard English speaker would use "at" ("I have to be there for one o'clock.")

fren - "friend."

fraid - "afraid."

frig, friggin, frig up - same as Standard English euphemism for "fuck" ("He talkin a heap ah frig", "meh computer frig up"). Can also mean "in a funny [wrong] way" ("She had watch me frig up" = "She was watching me in an odd way.")

fronting, frontin - (1) putting up a front, pretending ("She frontin like she couldn't solve some problem.") (2) slang verb for "up front" ("I decided to front all the money for this car and get it out the way.")

"from long" - used to mean "for a long time" ("I wuh late for the appointment i trying to geh from lang.") also: lang, lahng

fuck - can be used to refer to a thing ("Dat fuck brand new.")

"full up" - covered with ("Our skyut full up a green stain" = "Our skirts were stained green.")

fuss - "first" ("Leh we see who gon reach fuss.")

fustration - "frustration."

"finish" - used to mean "all out of," "all gone," "all done" ("Roti finish, meson.")

fyah - "fire."

G

"gahn een" - "gone in," someone who has gone crazy, lost his mind on drugs ("He gahn EEN, mehson.")

gane - "go" ("Leh we gane.") also: gan

ge, geh - pronunciation for "give/gave," "get, got" or "have/had" ("I gee he de ting.") also: gee

geit - pronunciation for "get/got it" ("Afta we geit, we pick up de tred from de kite and we stat walkin back" = "After we got it, we picked up the kite string and started walking back.")

gold digga - "gold digger," woman interested only in a man's money.

gon - pronunciation for "going to" or "gonna" ("Dey ain gon do dat.")

gongolo, gungalo - local name for millipedes (not to be confused with fast-moving centipedes which have a nasty bite, millipedes are the slow-moving rounded creatures that look like snippets of coaxial cable).

georgie bundle - a small bundle of possessions ("Pick up your georgie-bundle and geh out my house.")

"gettin a yout" - pregnant, having a baby.

"good to go" - ready.

"gone bush" - (1) expression to mean someone has disappeared into the bush, "gone back to nature" ("He gone bush, meson."), (2) something is missing ("Meh cellphone gone bush mehson.")

gran- (prefix) - "grand" ("granmuddah," "grandahtah," etc.)

gumption - slang for marijuana.

gyul - "girl."
also: gyal, gel, gyual

gyulfren - "girlfriend."

gwan - "going on" ("Wa gwan?")

H
ha - "had."

haas - pronunciation of "horse" ("He gotta heap ah haas-dem.")

hah - "her."

"hail up" - a greeting, like "Hi!"

"hall up" - wearing pants above the belly button , i.e. "hauled up."

halla, holla - literally "holler," meaning "get back to me" ("I busy so holla at me latah.")

hard-back - approaching middle age or older, old enough to know better ("So I tell he bout his hard-back ass and that he cannot give me no good sex.")

hata, hatas - literally, "hater, haters," from urban slang, meaning people who resent or are jealous, usually of someone else's success.

hata blockas - See "hata," urban slang for big, dark sunglasses that prevent the negative looks from haters getting through to the wearer.

haunted - used to mean terribly annoying ("You haunted de man!")

heap, heapa - "a lot" ("He mekkin a heap ah noise.")

heck - can be used to mean "thing."

hefa - a bitch; a disliked, overweight woman.

hello (HELlo) - used to get someone's attention.

herb, herbs - slang for marijuana.

"how [I, he/she] be" - used to indicate familiarity with someone's ways of behaving, as in "You dun know how I be."

huhs - pronunciation for "hers."

huhting, huttin - pronunciation for "hurting."

I

ignorant - used to refer to people who get "vex" quickly.

ih - "it" ("Ih real hot outside.")

Ine - "I ain't..." or "I don't..." ("Ine see dem" = "I didn't see them.")

"Inside!" - called out when visiting someone else's property.

Irie - okay, "cool."

I's - "I am ..." ("I's a Crucian!")

Isle, Isles - slang for "Sunny Isle Shopping Center ("Wanna go to isles?")

"it had" - substitution for "there was" ("November ah last year it had a big ting on de island mehson.")

iyo - "is everyone..." ("Iyo sleepin?")

izles, izzles (IZZles) - slang for "islands" ("A shout out to the BV Izles!" = "Hello to everyone in the Bristish Virgin Islands!")

J

Jack spaniard, spaniel - the particularly ill-tempered kind of wasp found on St. Croix ("A lot of jack spaniel sting me allova deman.") also: jacspania

jacked-up - messed up, bad. ("Fo real, dah bin a jacked-up day.")

jam - a party.

Jamaican tam - a hat for dreadlocks.

jean pants - where a statesider would say "jeans," a Crucian will say "jean pants."

"jive tru" - "drive through." ("When I deh in di Wendyz jive tru an look in my wallet, I had to tell de woman I comin back and tek a pass in by Banco wi my ATH cuz my pocket been huhting.")

jokey - describes someone who is silly, not serious.

jumbie - ghost, spirit.

K
kalaloo - a soup, used to mean a mix-up or disagreement, problem, fight ("I had to handle the situation on a professional level or there would of been a kalaloo up in the place.") also: kallaloo, callaloo

kasha (KAHsha) - acacia, a small tree with extremely long, sharp thorns.

"Kentucky" - what Crucians call "Kentucky Fried Chicken."

"kill me dead" - be hilarious, as in "She does kill me dead."

"Kill self with laugh" - literally, to kill oneself with laughter, to laugh so hard you might die ("When I read de card, I nearly kill self wid laff.")

knitting - slang for upset, concerned about the future ("I was in traffic for two hours so you dun know I knitting.")

knock, knack - "hit" ("Why you ain knock he fuss?")

kyat - a player of either sex, but especially used of males. See "pussman."

L
lahlah - idle gossip.

latah - "later" ("Wha you doin latah and so?")

lee - pronunciation for "leave" ("I gon lee ayo.")

lef - pronunciation for "left."

leh - "let/let's" ("Leh we go!")

licks - a beating ("We gato drive some lick in he rass toh cool he dung.")

"like peas" - an endless amount ("It have Othello like peas!")

lime - fun place to hang out, a party ("Wha pa de lime deh?")

limin, liming - relaxing, hanging out, going out ("Leh we gane limin no?")

"link up" - says both "goodbye" and "stay in touch" ("We'll link you up latah.")

loaftin - acting crazy ("She betta not come loaftin round me again.")

locks-up, lock up - (1) to grow dreadlocks ("He locksing up") or (2) possess dreadlocks ("Leh we go coop dem lock up dudes.")

long-side - "along side."

lyah - pronunciation for "liar."

lyrics - sweet lines uttered by flirtatious young men ("He start up wit his lyrics dem.")

M
"mad sick" - crazy ("On deh plane, turbulance was mad sick!")

mahnin - pronunciation for "morning" (Good mahnin!")
also: maning, marnin

magga - extremely skinny, starving, meager.
also: mahgah, meagah

My favorite street sign on St. Croix, at the intersection of 705 and 69, near Plessen and Estate Upper Love.

make - used where a Standard English speaker would use "turned," referring to a birthday ("she make six," meaning "she turned six years old.")

mama - female Puerto Rican ("Youza mama?")

mamaguy - to fool, trick or deceive ("I could try mamaguy my boyfriend for some money to go shopping.")

mampi (MOMpee) - "no see'ums," the seemingly invisible biting insects that emerge at sunset ("Mampis tearing me up, mehson!")

machete - (pronounced mahSHET), large hand-held blade used for cutting grass.

"mash up" - (1) wreck, ruin, tear up ("Sharri mash up she new car", "We go mash up de dance flah.") or (2) from music, a combination of different things ("She duh speak a mashup ah Crucian and Spanglish.")

mas - huge, magnificent ("Carnival in Cruz is mas!")

massive - a clique, i.e. Crucian Massive, Central High Massive, North Side Massive.

meen - "me ain't" run together, for "I don't." also: meain

meain know - (meAYno) Crucian for "I don't know." also: meaino, meeno, meh no

meh - "me."

mek, mekkin - "make," "making."

memba - pronunciation of "remember" ("Yoh memba she man, right?")

meson, mehson - literally "my son," used like "dude" or "oh, man!" might be used in the States, but does not refer exclusively to males or children. A ubiquitous interjection. "I late mehson" = "I'm late," "Mehson?" = "Tell me about it/no kidding!"

mih - "my."

melee (MEHlay) - gossip, scandal, crazy situation ("Gyul, you ain hear the melee that happen to me yesterday!")

mines - "mine" ("Da cyar ova deh gon be mines.")

mocko jumbie or moko jumbie - a popular Carnival figure, a masked, costumed person on stilts who scares away evil spirits.

much - often used when Standard English would call for "many" ("How much papah dem dis English class require?")

muddah - pronunciation for "mother" ("Weh yoh muddah deh? = "Where's your mother?")

"muddah land" - "motherland," usually refers to Africa.

muddahskunt - if you work this out phonetically, it is literally "mother's cunt," obviously an extremely rude, crass term, and it is often used exactly that way, the way Statesiders might use "motherfucker." If you use it, be sure you pronounce it correctly, (muddah-SKUNT), which like "rass" and "strupid" softens the effect slightly ("Geh yo muddaskunt!"). See also "skunt."

murderation - a difficult situation ("Afta she fadda had die, it was like murderation cuz she was so hurt, ya check?")

mussee - "must be/must have been" ("You mussee crazy!", "We end up leaving musi 7 o'clock in deh mahning.")
also: musi

N
nar - "not" ("He assumed dat ah did nar had my seatbelt on.")

natchuh ("nature") - male sexual drive

nerves - where a Standard English speaker would say "That guy had some nerve...", in Crucian it's "nerves."

nex, next - used for "another" ("Geh she a nex one" = "Get her another one.")

nene, neyney - grandmother.

"niggaritis" - the overwhelming feeling that a nap is needed after a big meal ("Afta she kill the kallaloo, niggaritis staht to click in: her rass ah sleepy bad.")

"no sa/sah" - "No, sir," to mean "Absolutely not."

nuff - "a lot of" ("Gyul, it had nuff cuties lined up fo dat foam party.")

nuffness - showiness, bravado ("So I take my nuffness gwan go ask the man for money.")

nuh - "no" ("Me ain see nuh man" = "I didn't see any men.")

nuttin - pronunciation for "nothing" ("I ain do nuttin.")
also: nuting

nyam - "eat" ("I nyaming my food.")
also: yam

nyampi (NYAM-pee) - the mucus secreted from the eyes, generally found upon waking in the morning, sometimes euphemistically referred to by Statesiders as "sleep" ("I wake up wid nyampi in meh eye," "I deck deh man a hard punch right in between he yampee eye dem.")
also: yampee

O
"off deh chain" - from urban slang, meaning "da bomb," really good, extremely attractive.

onliest - used to mean "only" ("Dat de onliest one.")

orda - pronunciation for "order."

P

pa, pah - used like "where" ("Pa she deh?" = "Where is she?")

pahtnah - "partner," friend or acquaintance, usually male ("He helpin he pahtnah," "I link up wi my pahtnah dem an just went Sharkey's.")
also: pawtnah, pardhah, partnah

Papa, papa - (1) male Puerto Rican ("Yousa Papa?" = "Are you Puerto Rican?"). (2) slang for "money" ("People bin spendin da papa foh dis ting.")

papeh - pronunciation for "paper" ("You know when skool almos ova when de teacha geh you a lang pepa to write.")
also: pepa

papis (paPEES) - men, usually Hispanic ("You shoulda see dem sexy Puerto Rican papis!")

para, parah - crazy or paranoid.

"peace out" - used as a farewell ("Peace out, man, an stay safe.")

peep game - "check it out," "let me tell you something": to inform a person of what's happening ("Peep game: this is how cris I break it down to her.")

peeps - my family, my people, from Stateside urban slang ("I went and visit my peeps by Concordia.")

pepe - grandfather.

picnee - children.
also: piknee, pickney

P.I.M.P. - "Playa Into Making Progress."

plainy - a joint composed of marijuana only.

popo - Stateside slang for "police" ("Deh popo dem staht drivin rung sehing ain got no more parking.")

"pop off" - like "go off" in Stateside slang, to go crazy/get violent ("I gon pop off on dem man.")

"poppin off" - slang for lots going on ("I reach deh and tings dun been poppin off.")

Preblo - sometime pronunciation of Pueblo grocery store ("I saw he pueen what had look like a Preblo bag" = "I saw him putting it in what looked like a Pueblo bag.")

Pueblo bag - used universally to refer to plastic grocery bags from any store on St. Croix.

pueen - pronunciation for "put it in."

Puerto-Crucian - someone of Puerto Rican descent born and/or raised on St. Croix. also: Cruzanrican

puss - girl.

pussman - a male player, one who is skilled at manipulating – "playing" – women by pretending to care about them, when in reality he is only interested in sex). See also "kyat."

putt putt, put put - old car.

Q

Quadrille - native dance of the Virgin Islands and other Caribbean islands, similar to square dancing, with traditional dress featuring madras fabrics.

quaht - short for "quarter," twenty-five cent coin.

qual - shortened form of "quarrel" ("Wha yo quallin fa?")

Quelbe - official music of the U.S. Virgin Islands, also known as "scratch music." Famous local groups include Stanley and the Ten Sleepless Knights, Bully and the Kafooners and Jamesie and the All-Stars.

R

raga, ragga - an old car.

rample - literally "rumple," to mess up ("Don rample up de bed I mek up mehson!")

Ras, ras - polite term of address to a Rastafarian.

rass - more polite way (sort of) of saying "ass" ("Yo rass GOOD, meson!", "I should call duh police fuh yorass!", "Move yo rass from round me!")

Rastaman - A male Rastafarian, can be used as a substitute for a name, ("Rastaman, how you is?")

reach - used to indicate arrival ("He ain reach yet?", "He reach to her house.")

redbone - a Black person with light skin ("Your boy jus bin coolin with a book in he hand when this foine looking redbone started rolling on me.")

ride - from Stateside slang, "car" (Dat ride cris, de man.")

rims up - adjective to describe a car with special wheel rims.

"rock stone" - these are separate terms to Statesiders, but one to Crucians (He windshield geh hit wid a rock stone.")

roll - from urban slang, to mean "outlook on life" ("You know how I does roll.")

rolling, rollin - to make a flirtatious or sexual advance.

"roll up" - to sneak up on someone, usually in a car ("You better be careful before Babylon roll up on you.")

rubba dem - sneakers ("You haven seen my rubbadem?")

run/runnin tings - expression used to indicate someone who is the boss, often used derisively ("He tink he runnin tings, mehson.")

runnings - errands, driving around ("I had to carry she round deh place to do her runnings.")

rung - pronunciation for "round," "around."
also: roung

S
Santo - Santo Domingan ("Yousa Santo?")

scale - device for weighing out marijuana.

seerias (emphasis on the "ee") - pronunciation for "serious."

self - often used in conjunction with a pronoun ("Meain self know" = "I don't know, myself", "you can self res" = "you can rest yourself.")

shame - used where Standard English speakers would use "ashamed" ("Afta dat, I feel shame.")

shanty (shanTEE) - bus stop shelter ("You won believe wah happen to we while walkin to deh shanty fo deh bus.")

sharp - good-looking ("Yoh sharp de man!")

sheen - (sheAIN) literally "she ain't" ("Sheen gon help you.")

shuga - "sugar," refers to diabetes.

shorty - from urban slang, a good-looking female.

"sick" - (1) borrowed from urban slang, used to mean "cool" or beautiful ("Dat cyar look sick!"), (2) can mean "crazy" ("Ayo man sick" = "You people are crazy.")

siddung - "sit down."

skanty - bicycle.

skeezer - slang for a woman with low morals and poor hygiene.

sket, skettel, sketty - a sexually promiscuous woman ("Of course you don know she a big sket askin me could I loan she some money.")

skunt - see "muddahskunt," literally a euphemism for "cunt,"extremely rude term ("Siddung and hush yoh skunt!")

skyatta - (pronunciation for "scatter" ("When it reach like 5 a.m. we skyatta, and I went home and knock out on de couch.")
also: scatta

skyut - pronunciation for "skirt."

slippas - literally "slippers," but refers to dress shoes.
also: slipas

"slow yuh roll" - used to mean "Now, just slow down a minute!"

"soon come" - coming soon ("Christmas soon come"), or as in "I'm coming back soon."

someting - pronunciation for "something."

"stop lie" - "stop lying" ("She tell me dis your new cyar and I say stop lie!")

strappin - carrying a concealed gun ("Keep it on the down low, but I'm strappin.")

strupid - euphemism for "stupid."
also: schupid, shupid, chupid

suck teeth - see "chupse."

suh - "such," commonly used as "and suh" at the end of a phrase ("She was all ova me giving me hugs an suh.")

swatcey - fat and slobby.

T

tambran - pronunciation for "tamarind" on St. Croix.

tan tan - *leucaena*, a common weed plant growing in the bush.

taught - pronunciation for "thought."
also: tat, taght

tek - pronunciation for "take" ("Tek weh yohsef" = "Get out of here.")

"The Bob" - short for "Babylon," used to refer specifically to the United States.

tief - (TEEF) literally "thief," used as a verb, i.e, "to steal" ("I teefin office papah.")
also: teef

tight-up - "tight" (Dat police come ova like he bad in he tight-up pants.")

ting - "thing."

tink - "think" ("He tink he betta dan she.")

touriss - (tourISSS) pronunciation for "tourist."

tree, t'ree - pronunciation for "three."

"trick" - refers to an unpleasant person, usually female ("Dis trick come steppin to me with a bunch of attitude when I was at work.")

trippin - from urban slang, used to mean overreacting, blowing small things out of proportion ("Dat bwoy still trippin.")

troupe - (pronounced TROOP), a group of performers, like the St. Croix Majorettes or UVI 4-H Club, who march in the Crucian Christmas Festival parades.

"true dat" - "That's true!"

tryna - "trying to."

tursty - "thirsty."
also: tusty

Twin City - refers to St. Croix, which has two towns, Christiansted and Frederiksted, while St. Thomas - "Rock" - has Charlotte Amalie and St. John - "Love City" - has Cruz Bay.

U
udda, uddah - pronunciation for "other."

V

vex - "angry" or "upset", used far more often in Crucian than in Standard English, where "vexed" is considered a bit old-fashioned ("I so vex at she", "Why you look so vex?")

vibe, vibes - atmosphere or feelings ("Dat deh was some real upsetting vibes, deh man."), can also refer to business dealings ("She would check a partner to deal wit dat vibes for hah.")

Virgin - Crucians pronounce this more like "VUHgin."

Virgin Islander - Emphasis can be on the second syllable "eyeLANDer."

W

Wa - "what" "wa gwan" = "what's going on?", see also used with "pa" to mean "where" ("Wha pa she deh" = "Where is she?"
also: wha, whepa

Wadadli Crucian - an Antiguan-Crucian, named for Antigua Brewery's "famous flagship" beer.

WAPA (WAHpa) - The Virgin Islands Water and Power Authority.

wais - pronunciation for "waist," but used to mean more than just the concept of "waist" – it may refer to the body from the waist down, especially during suggestive dancing.

"walk wid" - expression to mean carry something with you, bring it along ("She ain had no cinnamon, so I gon walk wid it.")

wapen - "what is happening?" or "What happened?"

wan, waan - "want" (You waan talk to he?")

watah - (waTAH) pronunciation for "water."

weed - marijuana

well - used as an adjective to indicate "extremely" ("a well-dead dahg.")

wes - west, as in the west side of St. Croix, Frederiksted ("Dem deh on the beach in Wes" = "They're on the beach on the West end.")

wha - "what."
also: wah

"Wha mek" - "why" ("Wha mek you do dat?")

"Wha mek you don't..." - expression for "Why don't you..." ("Wha make you don't like he?", "Wha mek you don't stop lie?")

whateva, whaeva - "whatever," often used as in Stateside slang, as a euphamistic indication of disagreement or lack of concern (Q: "You gon be dere?" A: "Whateva.")

whip - slang for "car" ("I had just got me a new whip ca I tyad a drivin ragas.")

whitey - White person.

whole - often pronounced "hoe," its meaning is the same as in Standard English but used differently in Crucian, in place of "the entire," as in "I bin wukkin whole day."

"whole heapa nar" - talking, communication with stupid suggestions, with lots of attitude, in a condescending tone ("He stat goin on wid a whole heapa nar.")

"Who da be?" - "Who is that?"

whoop - form of child descipline ("I gon whoop yoh lil rass.")

wicked - slang for "very good" ("Your new whip looks wicked.")

wid - pronunciation for "with" ("I study wid she.")

wine, wind, wine up - dance salaciously (You ain seen she wine she wais?")

wood - slang for penis.

wrang - pronunciation for "wrong."

wuk - "work" ("She aiin cum to wuk today.")

wuk up - to dance (usually specific to calypso or soca music).

wukking - "working at" ("Back den I was wukking Urban Threadz.")

wurn - "was/were not" ("He wurn deh.")

wus (WUSS) - "worst."

Y

ya, yah - here ("Dese pencil yah is yours?", "I deh yah coolin", "She live far from yah?")

yam - see nyam.

Yankee - person from the United States.

yankin' - a Crucian using Stateside-style Standard English.

"yoh ain know" - used where in Standard English "You won't believe" or "you'll never guess" might be used ("You ain know wha happen to me da uda day?")

"yoh doh hear!" - used for "you haven't heard?" ("Yoh doh hear! Weenie mash up his ride sick-sick on de highway.")

"yourass" - rude for "you."

"You dun know" - used for "Don't you know" or "you can be sure" ("So you dun know I throw she a couple of lines and geh she hooked man.")

yous - "you are."

yousa, yous a - (YOO-za) "Are you a..." "You are a..." ("Yousa Crucian", "Yous a papa?")

yout - (YOOT) pronunciation for "youth," young people.

yuh - "your" ("Wha hoppin to yuh foot?") also: yo, yoh

A Brief Linguistic History of St. Croix

Crucian creole goes back approximately 300 years, with beginnings around 1700. While St. Croix belonged to various European governments, most of the white settlers were English and Irish. Many of the settlers brought along slaves from the western coast of Africa, and they brought their native languages with them as well.

Whenever two distinct language groups encounter each other, a pidgin results. Pidgin is a vastly simplified mixture of two or more languages with a basic grammar and vocabulary. No one uses the pidgin as a first language; it is simply a basis for rudimentary communication. When, over time, children start learning the pidgin as their first language, and it eventually becomes the mother tongue of a community, it becomes a creole.

Over time on St. Croix, slaves from different regions in Africa with different languages, and the Europeans who interacted with them regularly, created an oral language, an English-based creole, with a rich vocabulary and discernable rules related to grammar and sentence structure (for a fascinating look at creole languages around the world, here's a great book: *Bastard Tongues: A Trail-Blazing Linguist Finds Clues to Our Common Humanity in the World's Lowliest Languages* by Derek Bickerton).

This language stabilized itself and was fairly pure until St. Croix was purchased by the United States in 1917 and Americans started moving to the island, along with an influx of natives from other Caribbean islands, who brought their own language patterns with them. Add the influences of TV, movies, hip-hop culture and music and the Internet, and it's easy to see why many linguists feel Virgin Islands Creole is a dying language. There's also a lot of social pressure put on Crucians to master Standard English as a route to educational and financial success.

But most young Crucians today are at ease shifting between Crucian and Standard English, and many are fluent in—and mix in words from—Spanish or Splanglish and other languages and dialects as well. Purists may decry the mixture of language influences that is today's Crucian dialect, but young Crucians celebrate "Cruzonics" as a rich, vibrant, living language.

Prehistory (5,000-1,000 years ago) to 1400: Paleo-Indians and Meso-Indians like the Ciboney (the word means "cave dweller" in Arawak) lived on St. Croix. We have no idea about their language, and no direct records of their lives or culture.

FAMIGLIA INDIANA CARAIBA.

Arawak-speaking people from South America then arrived in the area and inhabited St. Croix. Arawaks settled in villages and built round houses with timber walls and palm thatch roofs. Some Taino words we use today: iguana - lizard; tabacú - tobacco; canoa - canoe; cay - island.

1400: The Arawaks were driven out of St. Croix by Caribs, invading in long dugout canoes from the South. Invading Carib males often captured Arawak females to be their wives, resulting in a bilingual society. The Caribbean is named after the Caribs.

1493: On his second voyage, Christopher Columbus

"discovered" the Virgin Islands and Puerto Rico, naming the Virgin Islands for the legend of St. Ursula and her 11,000 virgin martyrs. He named our island Santa Cruz (Holy Cross). Salt River is the only positively documented site associated with Columbus' exploration of the New World on what is now a U.S. territory (so when we say "Columbus discovered America," we mean he discovered St. Croix!)

1507-1590: The Spanish on Puerto Rico first bargained with and then enslaved St. Croix's Caribs. Facing extermination, the Caribs abandoned St. Croix.

1600-1900: The languages of Europe—Spanish, English, French, Danish and Dutch—dominated the Virgin Islands, as these countries took turns settling and wresting control over the islands.

On St. Croix, the major European language spoken was English, beginning with a group of English-speaking people who had been living on St. Kitts and Barbados who tried to settle on St. Croix in 1630. The Spanish and French drove off the English as best they could, but English speakers kept coming back. It was reported that despite Danish ownership, St. Croix by 1741 had five times as many English settlers as Danes.

In 1673 the first consignment of 103 Africans arrived on St. Thomas to be sold into slavery. They were speakers of Kwa – not a single language, but a cluster of more than 100 languages spoken in Cote d'Ivoire, Ghana, Togo, Benin and Nigeria. Twi (Akan Ashanti from Ghana) is a Kwa language.

In order to communicate with each other and with the Europeans, slaves developed creoles. Creoles with a Dutch lexicon, Neggarhollands or "Negro Dutch Creole," emerged on St. Thomas and St. John. People on St. Croix spoke an English-based creole.

In 1841, the Danish islands received permission from Denmark to replace "Negro Dutch Creole" with English. Gov. Peter Von Scholten opened eight country schools on St. Croix to help prepare enslaved black children for freedom.

The Americanization of St. Croix first impacted language shortly after the islands were purchased by the U.S. in 1917, when officials made Standard English the official language of government and school, characterizing Crucian as "defective" and Standard English as "good English."

The Present: Today, English language everywhere is influenced by forces like television and film, the Internet and popular culture. St. Croix is no exception.

In the early to mid 1990's a humorous local newspaper, *The Island Melee*, ran what purported to be a summary of the previous week's episodes of the soap opera *All My Children* (so popular here it's rebroadcast in the evening so everyone can see it). "All My Chil'ren Dem" was written in Crucian and featured as much commentary as storyline: "An' wa bout all dem women goin' afta Noah? All a dem wan' some o dat sweet ting. Julie well know dat she wan' he, buh she playin' stchupid an' she'n wan ge he none. Well, leh she stand deh wid dat. Well chil', Taylor mus be done know bout how Rasta mon wan ting all day long, so run go geh he some. Buh' wait, dem locks on Noah head is real? To me it look like he ga a K-Mart mop 'pon he head."

The Tempo Channel, launched in 2005 by MTV as a compendium of music videos and interviews from all over the Caribbean, and founded by Crucian Frederick Morton, has opened a fast-changing world of creole and slang to a generation of pan-Caribbean youth.

In 2007, the St. Thomas campus of the University of the Virgin Islands was featured in the notorious fourth season of *College Hill* on the Black Entertainment Network. Four Virgin Islands students clashed and cavorted with four young

people from California. The network chose to screen Standard English subtitles for its mostly stateside audience when tempers rose and the Virgin Islands students' dialect got a little thick.

Look for *The Caribbean Writer*, the University of the Virgin Islands' annual literary magazine, for examples of creative writing in the languages of the Caribbean. Local bookstores sell many St. Croix history books, as well as fiction, poetry and memoirs written in Crucian.

Deh man, my muddascunt shoulda tried out for College Hill. Dey geh a buncha light skin bitchez and people from Bab. My fren dem say all I would do is cuss dem people on camera. True dat. Buh I woulda just been there to make it more real.

Acknowledgments

Dr. Arnold Highfield, UVI professor emeritus in Social Sciences and Linguistics, helped me more than I can say, identifying elements of linguistics the students and I could explore and sharing his expertise in Crucian Creole and the history of the Virgin Islands with my classes. His forthcoming definitive dictionary of classic old-school (pre-1917) Crucian Creole—with some 15,000 entries—will forever change the study of this language.

Marvin Williams, editor of *The Caribbean Writer* literary magazine and gifted writer—in Crucian—of short fiction, poetry and plays that celebrate St. Croix and its culture, was a source of wonder and inspiration in every class he visited and someone I respect immensely as a friend.

My best friend, Bethany Bradford, DVM, director of veterinary services for V.I. Agriculture, deserves recognition as the original inspiration for this project. I'll never forget her appearance in my writing classroom in Chicago, regaling my students with stories while code-switching among Standard English, her hilarious Maine accent (accourse!) and Crucian. I know everyone in that room remembers the story about the irate lady who drove up to Ariculcha on Rock and dropped off the "well-dead dahg."

Without Dr. David Gould, associate professor of English at UVI and (then) Humanities division chair, who patiently tolerated my whining about the focus ENG 201 had when I arrived in 2005 and eventually agreed I could remake the course as an extended project in intercultural communication, there would be nothing in your hands right now.

My husband Mitch Hennes introduced me to two wonderful artifacts that shaped this book. One is *Say it in Yiddish,* an exhaustive 1958 "phrase book for travelers" of a language you can't actually go anywhere where everyone is speaking it. The other is *How to Speak Hip* (1959), mock language acquisition lessons by Del Close and John Brent, in which a totally cool hipster demonstrates slang to an impossibly square speaker of Standard English (the words "like," "man," and "dig," are the keys to basic spoken Hip. "I'm going to the post office" becomes "Like, I'm going to the post office, man. You dig?") This hilarious album (hear it at www. howtospeakhip.com) inspired the decidedly unhip "translations" in this book.

Finally, and most importantly, my students.

Special thanks to Anika Johnson for agreeing to share her wonderful story, "Visitation," and to Miguelina Valdes for "Crucian Cinderella."

On the following page, the students whose ENG 201 work I saved, referred to and quoted from in this book. Much of the content is theirs, including the conversations and sentences reproduced throughout the book, and most of the dictionary definitions. I'm still astonished at how hard these students worked to conduct original research— interviewing their friends, siblings, parents and grandparents, to write Crucian versions of fairytales, to retell their own stories, and to thoughtfully analyze a language most of them had never considered in this way before.

To all my students at UVI: I love you and miss you every day. It was a privilege to be your teacher.

Dr. S

Shama Abbott
Sonja A. Acosta
Shenell Albert
Almaza Ali
Jenelle Alsuran
Megan Buchanan
Angela Boateng
Laurna Bodley
Scott Cave
Merlice Charles
Rose Marie Charles
Mufasa Carl A.
    Christopher
Shanella Clarke
Saskia Corke
Tanisia Corke
Victoria Cornelius
Caesy Cuffy
Maribel Cruz
Carl Derricks
LaMar Doward
Dawn Drew
Amanda Dunstan
Somalia Edwards
Rochelle Elizee
Kyria Fawkes
Karolyn Marie Felix
Eva Francis
Maisha Frederick
Irene Garcia
Carolyn Gonsales
David Mustafa Gross
Denise Halverson
Nadil Hamad
Sana W. Hamed
Dwayne Harvey
Alanna Hayden
Kai Hayes
Erma Heyliger
Kareema Huggins
Shawnte Isaac
O'keffe Jacobs
Kennalyne Jn Baptiste

Omar Jarvis
Kai Joseph
Trinisia Jones
Mutahammis Kareem
Kevin Labadie
Kemi Lay
Apreel Lubin
Denis R. Lynch II
Ana Maria Montanez
Debra P. Miller
Malkia Morton
Carmen Navarro
Shareen Neale
Tiffonee Nicholas
David F. Obando
Jelani Osborne
Yania Pellicer-Carmona
Kim Phillip-St. Hall
Lynesha Sweeney
Felicia Polydore
Flerida Quezada
Irene Ramos
Melanie Ruiz
Kamal Russell
Maricella Sanes
Donela Shillingford
Rudi Shulterbrandt
Daneeze Silcott
Patricia Speakman
Bernhardt Simmonds
Shunda Simon
Gisel Saldaña
Jamal Soldiew
Andrea Soto
Lynesha Sweeney
Marelle Sylvester
Tamisha I. Thomas
Renesha Urgent
Luna L. William
Shervin Williams
Tiffany Williams
Miguelina Valdes
Andres E. Velazquez